Make a New Friend in Jesus

PassAlong Arch® Books help you share Jesus with friends close to you and with children all around the world!

When you've enjoyed this story, pass it along to a friend. When your friend is finished, mail this book to the address below. Concordia Gospel Outreach promises to deliver your book to a boy or girl somewhere in the world to help him or her learn about Jesus.

Myself

My name _____

My address _____

_____

My PassAlong Friend

My name _____

My address _____

When you're ready to give your PassAlong Arch® Book to a new friend who doesn't know about Jesus, mail it to

Concordia Gospel Outreach
3547 Indiana Avenue
St. Louis, MO 63118

PassAlong Series

Copyright © 1995 Concordia Publishing House
3558 S. Jefferson Avenue, St. Louis, MO 63118-3968
Manufactured in the United States of America

1 2 3 4 5 6 7 8 9 10   04 03 02 01 00 99 98 97 96 95

Daniel in the Dangerous Den

Daniel 1–6; Psalm 137:1–6
for Children

Carol Greene
Illustrated by Michelle Dorenkamp

SAINT LOUIS

 young man called Daniel was taken away
With others from Judah one sorrowful day.
Their country was conquered,
    their government gone,
And they went as exiles to far Babylon.

"Being taken from your home is no fun."

Come, sing something joyful,"
their captors declared.
But those songs were sacred and not to
be shared.
"Our hearts are too heavy. You must understand.
We can't sing our Lord's songs in some
foreign land."

And there by the waters they sat down
and wept.
"No matter what happens, we will not forget.
Our harps may be silent, our voices be still,
But God and our homeland, remember
we will."

"They'll remember.
Wait and see..."

Now Daniel was honest and handsome
and smart,
And love for the Lord always burned in
his heart.
As years passed he helped some of
Babylon's kings,
Explaining their nightmares and other
strange things.

The grateful kings dressed him in purple
and gold,
And gave him more power, till Daniel controlled
A lot of his captors. That made them see red.
"We'd be better off if that Daniel were dead."

"I once had a nightmare that I was a belt!"

King Darius trusted in Daniel so much,
He had him rule satraps and bigwigs
and such.
And then the king said, "I should put him
in charge
Of *all* of my kingdom. I'll do it, by George!"

And that's when the bigwigs and satraps
said, "Look!
We must stop this Daniel by hook or by
crook.
An investigation we must undertake
And see if we can't find some tiny mistake."

"Nasty folk!"

They searched Daniel's records and files all
    day long.
They asked his assistants, "What has he
    done wrong?"
They scrutinized scrolls till their eyeballs
    turned red,
And, some say, they even looked under
    his bed.

Their search was in vain, because Daniel
    was good.
He knew what was right, and he did what
    he should.
So then all the bigwigs and satraps began
To hatch in their heads a detestable plan.

"I wouldn't put anything past them!"

O King, live forever!" They scraped and
        they bowed.
"We have an idea, and we think you'll be
        proud
To make it a law that nobody can break,
A law carved in stone for your glorious sake.

"O King, live forever! When anyone prays,
It must be to you for the next thirty days.
Whoever does not, will avoid jail and fines.
He'll simply be tossed in a den full of lions."

"Careful,
Darius!
    It's a trick."

All right," said the king, and he wrote down the law.

His own self-importance was all that he saw.

But when Daniel heard it, he just shook his head.

"Poor king (live forever!)—he has been misled."

Then Daniel went home, and he looked to the west

And thought of the times each day that he loved best,

When he faced his homeland and prayed to his God.

"Me, pray to the King? That would surely seem odd.

"Imagine praying to a measly old king!"

I'll pray to no king," Daniel said. "No not I!
   I'll pray to the Lord even if I must die.
   For my God, the true God, remembers me
      still,
   And I will remember and follow His will."

And so three times daily he knelt down
      and prayed
In front of the windows. He was not afraid.
Then one day the bigwigs and satraps
      sneaked past.
"It's Daniel. He's praying. We've got him at
      last!"

"See? Daniel remembered God."

OKing, live forever! Just guess what
    we've found.
It's someone who's praying, his knees on
    the ground.
It's Daniel, and he is not praying to you.
So sad. Live forever! Now what will you do?"

"You tricked me!" The king turned dark
    purple with rage.
"I should have known better, a man of my
    age.
But I will save Daniel. I'll figure a way."
"You have," they said sweetly, "the rest of
    the day."

"Come on, king. Figure a way!"

King Darius struggled. He clutched at each straw.
But even the king could not strike down
    his law.
"It's evening," the men said. "Though you
    love him so,
The lions want their dinner, and Daniel
    must go."

So Daniel was brought, and the king bowed
    his head.
"I hope that your God will protect you," he said.
"You serve Him each day, and He must
    hold you dear.
Perhaps He can help you. I'm helpless, I fear."

"I'm *sure*
God will
help Daniel."

And Daniel was thrown in the lions' den at last,
A stone set before it to keep it shut fast,
And seals on the stone that nobody could
     break.
The king went to bed, where he lay wide awake.

"What must they be doing, those fierce
     beasts?" he thought.
"Is Daniel still running, or has he been caught?
Or has he been eaten clear down to his bones?"
The king's bedroom rang with the king's
     moans and groans.

"Darius had
a bad,
bad night!"

As soon as the first light of dawn lit the sky,
  King Darius woke the whole town with
    his cry.
"O Daniel, did your God help you to survive?
Dear Daniel, please answer me! Are you
    still alive?"

"O King, live forever! I certainly am.
My God helped me out of this terrible jam.
Those fierce wild beasts purred at the angel
    He sent,
And kept their mouths shut through the
    whole incident."

"Hooray!"

Then Daniel came out, and the king heaved
      a sigh,
And, some say, the littlest lion waved good-bye.
The bigwigs and satraps had nothing to say.
Those fierce wild beasts ate them for breakfast
      that day.

"I'm planning," said Daniel, "to give thanks
      to God.
O King, live forever." The king gave a nod.
"I'm making a new law," he cheerfully said.
"That old one was stupid. It's now null
      and dead."

"Atta boy, Darius!"

"God is everywhere, you know."

Throughout all the land the king sent his
    new law:
    "From now on, treat Daniel's God with fear
        and with awe,
    For He is the true God. His kingdom won't end.
    And on all who worship Him, blessings
        He'll send."

So Daniel went back to his work for the king,
Still far from his homeland, but he knew
    one thing—
Wherever he traveled, whatever the spot,
His God was there. That Daniel never forgot.

When problems and hurts are like fierce beasts
to you,
Remember, like Daniel, that you can pray
too.
Your God hears the quietest words in your
head
And turns all the fierce things to blessings
instead.

"You can pray anytime, anyplace. You can!"